# Jesse Tree
# Daily Devotions

Deaconess Michelle Domin

CONCORDIA PUBLISHING HOUSE • SAINT LOUIS

# Stump with a Shoot
### READING: ISAIAH 11

There shall come forth a shoot from the stump of Jesse, and a branch from his roots shall bear fruit.
(Isaiah 11:1)

It's December! We know what that means: Christmas is coming! Waiting is hard. It is hard to wait for the joy, the laughter, the family time, the food, and the presents. But why do we celebrate Christmas? We celebrate Christmas because we celebrate Christ. Jesus, who is true God, begotten of the Father from eternity, came down from heaven and became a little baby boy. He lived, died, and rose again, that our sins would be washed away and we would live with Him forever.

Waiting is hard. Before Jesus was born, a lot of people were waiting for the Messiah. God promised Jesse's son, King David, that the Messiah would be his descendant. The Messiah would be a part of Jesse's family tree. The people of Israel anxiously awaited the arrival of the promised Messiah, just as we are now waiting to celebrate the birth of Jesus this Christmas. Jesus is the branch that bears fruit from the stump of Jesse, and we, as baptized children of God, are grafted into the branch. We are a part of God's family tree! During this Advent and Christmas season, we will follow the promise of the Messiah, from creation to the events surrounding Jesus' birth.

# The World
### READING: GENESIS 1:1–2:4

God saw everything that He had made, and behold, it was very good.

(Genesis 1:31a)

In the beginning, God created the heavens and the earth by the power of His word. He said, "Let there be light," and there was light. All of creation—aside from man—was made when God spoke it into being. Man was made with dust, water, and the breath of God. In six days, He created the world and everything in it, and on the seventh day, God rested. He looked at everything He had made, and it was very good. The mountains, trees, stars, animals, and all of creation reflected God's majesty. Man was made in God's image. Everything was perfect.

### "At the Name of Jesus"

At the name of Jesus Ev'ry knee shall bow,
Ev'ry tongue confess Him King of glory now.
'Tis the Father's pleasure We should call Him Lord,
Who from the beginning Was the mighty Word.

At His voice creation Sprang at once to sight,
All the angel faces, All the hosts of light,
Thrones and bright dominions, Stars upon their way,
All the heav'nly orders In their great array.

(*LSB* 512:1–2)

# Apple

READING: GENESIS 2:7–25; 3:1–24

When the woman saw that the tree was good for food, and that it was a delight to the eyes, and that the tree was to be desired to make one wise, she took of its fruit and ate, and she also gave some to her husband who was with her, and he ate.

(Genesis 3:6)

Although God made a perfect world, it did not stay perfect for long. Adam and Eve disobeyed God when they ate from the tree of the knowledge of good and evil. Sin entered the world, and with it, death. God still loved His creation, and He gave Adam and Eve the promise of a Savior. God said to Satan, "And I will put enmity between you and the woman, and between your offspring and her offspring; He shall bruise your head, and you shall bruise His heel" (Genesis 3:15). This was the first Gospel promise. Jesus was the offspring that would destroy Satan through His death on the cross.

### "Creator of the Stars of Night"

Creator of the stars of night,
Thy people's everlasting Light:
O Christ, Redeemer, save us all
And hear Thy servants when they call.

Thou, grieving that the ancient curse
Should doom to death a universe,
Hast found the healing, full of grace,
To cure and save our ruined race.

(*LSB* 351:1–2)

# Rainbow
### READING: GENESIS 6–9

**KEY BIBLE VERSE**

And God said, "This is the sign of the covenant that I make between Me and you and every living creature that is with you, for all future generations: I have set My bow in the cloud, and it shall be a sign of the covenant between Me and the earth."

(Genesis 9:12–13)

The world became very sinful after Adam and Eve disobeyed God. It became so bad that Noah and his family were the only people who were still faithful. God destroyed the world with a flood, but He saved Noah and his family in the ark. God's promise of a Savior would continue through their family. When we see a rainbow, we can remember God's promise to never destroy the world by water again. We can also remember that just as sin was destroyed in the flood, our sins were destroyed in the waters of Holy Baptism.

### "Water, Blood, and Spirit Crying"

In a wat'ry grave are buried
All our sins that Jesus carried;
Christ, the Ark of Life, has ferried
	Us across death's raging flood.

(*LSB* 597:2)

# Tent

READING: GENESIS 12:1–3

KEY BIBLE VERSE:

And I will make of you a great nation, and I will bless you and make your name great, so that you will be a blessing.

(Genesis 12:2)

God did not forget His promise of a Savior to Adam and Noah. He chose to continue the promise through a man named Abraham. God asked Abraham to move to a new land, and Abraham trusted in the Lord, even when he was living in a tent and did not know where he was going. God promised Abraham that he would be the father of a great nation. Abraham would have so many offspring that counting them would be like trying to count the stars in the sky. His descendants became the nation of Israel, God's chosen people, and from Israel came our Savior, Jesus Christ.

### "The God of Abraham Praise"

The God of Abr'ham praise, Whose all-sufficient grace
Shall guide me all my pilgrim days In all my ways.
He deigns to call me friend; He calls Himself my God.
And He shall save me to the end Through Jesus' blood.

(*LSB* 798:3)

# Ram

### READING: GENESIS 22:1–14

**KEY BIBLE VERSE**

And Isaac said to his father Abraham, "My father!" And he said, "Here I am, my son." He said, "Behold, the fire and the wood, but where is the lamb for a burnt offering?" Abraham said, "God will provide for Himself the lamb for a burnt offering, my son."

(Genesis 22:7–8a)

Abraham and his wife, Sarah, had a son, Isaac, just as the Lord had promised. God tested Abraham by asking him to offer his only son as a burnt offering. In great faith, Abraham obeyed God. Yet God sent an angel to Abraham, saying, "Do not lay your hand on the boy or do anything to him, for now I know that you fear God, seeing you have not withheld your son, your only son, from Me" (Genesis 22:12). God provided a ram in the thicket for Abraham and Isaac to offer to the Lord. Just like Abraham, God did not withhold His only Son, Jesus Christ. Just like the ram, Jesus is the Lamb of God, who took our place when He died on the cross.

### "Not All the Blood of Beasts"

Not all the blood of beasts On Jewish altars slain
Could give the guilty conscience peace Or wash away the stain.

But Christ, the heav'nly Lamb, Takes all our sins away;
A sacrifice of nobler name And richer blood than they.

(*LSB* 431:1–2)

# Ladder

READING: GENESIS 28:10–22

**KEY BIBLE VERSE**

And behold, the LORD stood above it and said, "I am the LORD, the God of Abraham your father and the God of Isaac. The land on which you lie I will give to you and to your offspring. Your offspring shall be like the dust of the earth, and you shall spread abroad to the west and to the east and to the north and to the south, and in you and your offspring shall all the families of the earth be blessed."

(Genesis 28:13–14)

The promise of a Savior continued from Isaac to his son Jacob. One night, Jacob was traveling and slept outdoors with a rock for a pillow. He dreamed about a ladder that stretched from heaven to earth, with angels ascending and descending on it. The Lord was at the top, and He promised Jacob that all the families of the earth would be blessed from his offspring. That offspring was Jesus Christ. When Jesus died, He bridged the gap from heaven to earth. The cross acted like the ladder in Jacob's dream, reconciling the world to God. All the families of the earth are blessed through this ultimate sacrifice.

### "O Savior, Rend the Heavens Wide"

O Father, light from heaven send;
As morning dew, O Son, descend.
Drop down, you clouds, the life of spring:
To Jacob's line rain down the King.

(*LSB* 355:2)

# Coat of Many Colors
READING: GENESIS 37:12–36; 45:4–14

KEY BIBLE VERSE

So Joseph said to his brothers, "Come near to me, please." And they came near. And he said, "I am your brother, Joseph, whom you sold into Egypt. And now do not be distressed or angry with yourselves because you sold me here, for God sent me before you to preserve life."

(Genesis 45:4–5)

Jacob had twelve sons, and the one who continued the promise of a Savior was Judah. Yet Joseph was another son who played an important part in preserving that promise. Jacob loved Joseph best, and he gave him a coat of many colors. Joseph's brothers were jealous and sold him into slavery in Egypt. But God was with Joseph, and he became a great ruler. When famine struck, Joseph was able to provide food and save many people, including his own family. God had a plan for Joseph and used the bad things in his life for good. God has a plan for you and me as well. When something bad happens, we can trust in God because He gave us the best gift of all—salvation through Jesus Christ.

### "Through Jesus' Blood and Merit"

There's nothing that can sever From this great love of God;
No want, no pain whatever, No famine, peril, flood.
Though thousand foes surround me, For slaughter mark
 His sheep,
They never shall confound me, The vict'ry I shall reap.

(*LSB* 746:2)

# Ten Commandments

### READING: EXODUS 15:1–21

**KEY BIBLE VERSE:**

The LORD is my strength and my song, and He has become my salvation; this is my God, and I will praise Him, my father's God, and I will exalt Him.

(Exodus 15:2)

Another person who is not in the family tree of Jesus but who played an important part in preserving it is Moses. When the Israelites became slaves in Egypt, God used Moses to tell Pharaoh to let His people go. God saved them from slavery when they crossed the Red Sea on dry ground, and the Israelites praised God. When Moses was leading the Israelites, God gave them the Ten Commandments on stone tablets to tell them how to live their lives. The Israelites did not follow the Ten Commandments very well, and neither do we. We are slaves to sin, and God saves us through the waters of Holy Baptism. We can thank and praise God for our salvation, just as Moses did after crossing the Red Sea.

### "O Come, O Come, Emmanuel"

O come, O come, Thou Lord of might,
Who to Thy tribes on Sinai's height
In ancient times didst give the Law
In cloud and majesty and awe.

Rejoice! Rejoice! Emmanuel
Shall come to thee, O Israel!

(*LSB* 357:3)

# Grapes

### READING: NUMBERS 13

**KEY BIBLE VERSE**

And they told him, "We came to the land to which you sent us. It flows with milk and honey, and this is its fruit."

(Numbers 13:27)

God not only promised a Savior to Abraham, Isaac, and Jacob, but He also promised them a land flowing with milk and honey. God kept His promise and used Moses to lead the Israelites to the Promised Land. Even when the Israelites doubted God, He still gave them the gift of a wonderful land. The bunches of grapes were so big that two people were needed to carry one bunch! Even when we doubt God, He pours out His blessings upon us. His blessings are greater than we can even imagine.

### "The God of Abraham Praise"

Though nature's strength decay, And earth and hell
   withstand,
To Canaan's bounds I urge my way At His command.
The wat'ry deep I pass, With Jesus in my view,
And through the howling wilderness My way pursue.

The goodly land I see, With peace and plenty blest:
A land of sacred liberty And endless rest.
There milk and honey flow, And oil and wine abound,
And trees of life forever grow With mercy crowned.

(*LSB* 798:5–6)

# Sheaf of Wheat
### READING: RUTH 4

**KEY BIBLE VERSE**

Then the women said to Naomi, "Blessed be the LORD, who has not left you this day without a redeemer, and may his name be renowned in Israel!"
(Ruth 4:14)

The Israelites were God's chosen people, but He did not forget about the other nations. God chose Ruth, a woman who was not an Israelite, to be in Jesus' family tree. Ruth's husband died, but Ruth was faithful to her mother-in-law, Naomi, who was an Israelite. She said to Naomi, "Your people shall be my people, and your God, my God" (Ruth 1:16). God used a man named Boaz to help Naomi and Ruth, who were very poor. Boaz provided extra sheaves of wheat for Ruth to collect because he cared about her physical needs. Boaz married Ruth, and they had a son named Obed. Just as Boaz took care of Ruth and Naomi, God provides and cares for us, both physically and spiritually.

#### "Entrust Your Days and Burdens"

Entrust your days and burdens
  To God's most loving hand;
He cares for you while ruling
  The sky, the sea, the land.
For He who guides the tempests
  Along their thund'rous ways
Will find for you a pathway
  And guide you all your days.

(*LSB* 754:1)

# Shepherd's Staff
### READING: 1 SAMUEL 17

KEY BIBLE VERSE

[Jesus said,] "I am the good shepherd. The good shepherd lays down His life for the sheep."

(John 10:11)

Ruth's son, Obed, had a son named Jesse, and Jesse had a son named David. David was a shepherd boy, and he took good care of his sheep. God had big plans for David. He used him to defeat the giant Goliath and save the people of Israel. David cared greatly for his sheep and always protected them. Jesus is called the Good Shepherd. We are Jesus' sheep, and He loves us so much that He laid down His life for us by dying on the cross. He saved us, His sheep, from sin and death, just as David saved his sheep from lions and bears.

### "The King of Love My Shepherd Is"

The King of love my shepherd is,
   Whose goodness faileth never;
I nothing lack if I am His
   And He is mine forever.

Perverse and foolish oft I strayed,
   But yet in love He sought me
And on His shoulder gently laid
   And home rejoicing brought me.

(*LSB* 709:1, 3)

# Crown

READING: 2 SAMUEL 7:1–17

KEY BIBLE VERSE

And your house and your kingdom shall be made sure forever before Me. Your throne shall be established forever.

(2 Samuel 7:16)

God chose the shepherd boy David to be the king of Israel. David was a good king who followed the Lord. God promised David that his throne would be established forever. Many, many years later, that promise came true in Jesus Christ. Jesus is a descendant of King David, and He is the King of kings. He wore a crown of thorns, and the cross was His throne. Now Jesus sits at the right hand of God in glory, and He will be our King forever because of His great love for us.

### "Hail to the Lord's Anointed"

Hail to the Lord's anointed, Great David's greater Son!
Hail, in the time appointed, His reign on earth begun!
He comes to break oppression, To set the captive free,
To take away transgression And rule in equity.

Kings shall fall down before Him And gold and incense bring;
All nations shall adore Him, His praise all people sing.
To Him shall prayer unceasing And daily vows ascend;
His kingdom still increasing, A kingdom without end.

(*LSB* 398:1, 4)

# Temple
### READING: 1 KINGS 3:5–28

**KEY BIBLE VERSE**

Behold, I give you a wise and discerning mind, so that none like you has been before you and none like you shall arise after you. I give you also what you have not asked, both riches and honor, so that no other king shall compare with you, all your days.

(1 Kings 3:12b–13)

King David's son Solomon is famous for his God-given wisdom as well as his riches and honor. Solomon used some of his riches to build a temple for God. It was the place where God chose to dwell among His people. When Jesus came to earth, He became the new temple—the new place where God dwelt with man. Jesus told the Jews, "'Destroy this temple, and in three days I will raise it up.' The Jews then said, 'It has taken forty-six years to build this temple, and will You raise it up in three days?'" (John 2:19–20). The Jews had Solomon's temple in mind, but Jesus was talking about His body. He died on the cross, but He rose from the grave three days later. At the time of His death, the temple curtain tore in two, from top to bottom. This was God's way of showing that He no longer needed to dwell in the temple, because Jesus, true God, came to dwell among men.

### "Built on the Rock"

Surely in temples made with hands
  God, the Most High, is not dwelling;
High above earth His temple stands,
  All earthly temples excelling.
Yet He who dwells in heav'n above
Chooses to live with us in love,
  Making our bodies His temple.

(*LSB* 645:2)

16

# Scroll

READING: 2 KINGS 22:1–23:25

KEY BIBLE VERSE

Before him there was no king like him, who turned to the LORD with all his heart and with all his soul and with all his might, according to all the Law of Moses, nor did any like him arise after him.

(2 Kings 23:25)

King Josiah was a descendant of David and a part of Jesus' family tree. When he was king of Judah, the Book of the Law had been lost for a long time and the people did not know or follow God's Word. They worshiped false idols and were full of sin. Josiah was having the temple cleaned when he found the Book of the Law. When he read it, he realized just how evil God's chosen people had become. Josiah brought the Word of God back to the people, burned the false idols they were worshiping, and attempted to rid the land of evil. He also restored the celebration of Passover, which hadn't been celebrated in a long time. While Josiah temporarily displaced evil, Jesus conquered evil once and for all when He died on the cross.

**"A Great and Mighty Wonder"**

All idols then shall perish
And Satan's lying cease,
And Christ shall raise His scepter,
Decreeing endless peace.

(*LSB* 383:5)

# Fiery Altar
## READING: 1 KINGS 18:19–39

KEY BIBLE VERSE:

Elijah the prophet came near and said, "O Lᴏʀᴅ, God of Abraham, Isaac, and Israel, let it be known this day that You are God in Israel, and that I am Your servant, and that I have done all these things at Your word."

(1 Kings 18:36)

Although the prophet Elijah is not actually a part of Jesus' family tree, God used Elijah to prove to the prophets of Baal and all the people that the God of Israel is the true God. When the people saw how Elijah's sacrifice and altar were consumed by the fire of the Lord, they fell on their faces and said, "The Lᴏʀᴅ, He is God; the Lᴏʀᴅ, He is God" (1 Kings 18:39). While the people of Israel continued to turn away from God, God remembered His covenant with them. He gave a sacrifice even more worthy than Elijah's—His only Son, Jesus Christ. Jesus was the sacrifice, and the cross was His altar. Through that sacrifice, God paid for the sins of the whole world, and through Christ's resurrection we, too, can proclaim, "The Lᴏʀᴅ, He is God; the Lᴏʀᴅ, He is God."

### "Sing Praise to God, the Highest Good"

All who confess Christ's holy name,
  Give God the praise and glory.
Let all who know His pow'r proclaim
  Aloud the wondrous story.
Cast ev'ry idol from its throne,
For God is God, and He alone:
  To God all praise and glory!

(*LSB* 819:5)

# Watchtower

READING: MICAH 5:2–5

KEY BIBLE VERSE

But you, O Bethlehem Ephrathah, who are too little
to be among the clans of Judah, from you shall come
forth for Me one who is to be ruler in Israel, whose
coming forth is from of old, from ancient days.
(Micah 5:2)

Habakkuk and Micah were also prophets of God. They spoke His Word, and they foretold the coming of Jesus. Like many in Israel, they were waiting for the promised Savior. Habakkuk compared himself to a watchman, waiting for the Anointed One. He said, "I will take my stand at my watchpost and station myself on the tower" (Habakkuk 2:1a). Christmas is getting closer, but we are still waiting. Habakkuk knew that the coming of Jesus was getting closer, but he, too, had to continue waiting. Micah foretold that Jesus would be born in Bethlehem. After Jesus was born, it was the words of the prophet Micah that informed King Herod and the Wise Men where to find Him.

### "Rejoice, Rejoice, Believers"

The watchers on the mountain
   Proclaim the Bridegroom near;
Go forth as He approaches
   With alleluias clear.
The marriage feast is waiting;
   The gates wide open stand.
Arise, O heirs of glory;
   The Bridegroom is at hand.

(*LSB* 515:2)

# City Wall
### READING: DANIEL 6:2–29

KEY BIBLE VERSE

"My God sent His angel and shut the lions' mouths, and they have not harmed me, because I was found blameless before Him; and also before you, O king, I have done no harm."

(Daniel 6:22)

Even with a king like Josiah and prophets like Elijah who told the people to abandon their idols and pray to the Lord, the Israelites did not listen. God allowed them to be captured and go into exile in Babylon. Daniel was a prophet whom God raised up in Babylon, and God showed His power by keeping Daniel safe in the lions' den. Daniel had a dream about the coming Messiah as a king with dominion over all peoples, nations, and languages.

While they were still waiting for the Messiah, God brought His people back to Jerusalem, where they began to rebuild the city wall. The city wall reminds us that Jesus is the King with an everlasting dominion. We have to wait six more days to celebrate the birth of our King. The people of Israel would wait another four hundred years.

### "Lift Up Your Heads, Ye Mighty Gates"

Lift up your heads, ye mighty gates!
Behold, the King of glory waits.
The King of kings is drawing near;
The Savior of the world is here.
Life and salvation He doth bring;
Therefore rejoice and gladly sing.
To God the Father raise
Your joyful songs of praise.

(*LSB* 340:1)

# "His Name Is John"

READING: LUKE 1:5–25, 57–79

But the angel said to him, "Do not be afraid, Zechariah, for your prayer has been heard, and your wife Elizabeth will bear you a son, and you shall call his name John."

(Luke 1:13)

Zechariah and Elizabeth were without children, yet God gave them one in their old age. The angel Gabriel promised Zechariah that his child would prepare the way for the Lord. When Zechariah questioned that promise, he lost the ability to talk. When the baby was born, Zechariah wrote "His name is John" on a tablet, and his voice was restored. While Elizabeth was pregnant, her baby leaped in her womb when Mary, the mother of Jesus, came to visit. Elizabeth was filled with the Holy Spirit and exclaimed that Mary was the mother of her Lord. God showed His power by blessing Zechariah and Elizabeth with a child, and He gave them the gift of being among the first to know that the wait for the Messiah was over.

### "When All the World Was Cursed"

Before he yet was born, He leaped in joyful meeting,
Confessing Him as Lord Whose mother he was greeting.
By Jordan's rolling stream, A new Elijah bold,
He testified of Him Of whom the prophets told.

(*LSB* 346:2)

# Baptismal Shell
### READING: MARK 1:1–11

KEY BIBLE VERSE

And he preached, saying, "After me comes He who is mightier than I, the strap of whose sandals I am not worthy to stoop down and untie. I have baptized you with water, but He will baptize you with the Holy Spirit."

(Mark 1:7–8)

John the Baptist, the son of Zechariah and Elizabeth, was the last prophet to tell of the coming Messiah. He was given the spirit of Elijah, and he prepared the people for Jesus by preaching and baptizing in the Jordan River. At the beginning of Christ's ministry, John had the honor of baptizing Him. In that river, Jesus stood in the place of sinners and began His journey toward the cross. When we are baptized, we are united with Christ's death and resurrection. Our sins are washed away, and we become children of the heavenly Father.

### "When All the World Was Cursed"

When all the world was cursed By Moses' condemnation,
Saint John the Baptist came With words of consolation.
With true forerunner's zeal The greater One he named,
And Him, as yet unknown, As Savior he proclaimed.

O grant, dear Lord of love, That we receive, rejoicing,
The word proclaimed by John, Our true repentance voicing,
That gladly we may walk Upon our Savior's way
Until we live with Him In His eternal day.

(*LSB* 346:1, 4)

# Angel

READING: LUKE 1:26–38

In the sixth month the angel Gabriel was sent from God to a city of Galilee named Nazareth, to a virgin betrothed to a man whose name was Joseph, of the house of David. And the virgin's name was Mary.
(Luke 1:26–27)

God used the angel Gabriel as a messenger to bring good news, first to Zechariah and Elizabeth and then to Mary. An angel also came to Joseph in a dream, and a whole host of angels announced the good news of Christ's birth to the shepherds. Angels were also at the empty tomb on Easter morning to announce the glorious news that Jesus is alive. Just as God used angels to announce the coming of Jesus, He will also use angels to announce when Jesus is coming back on the Last Day. Jesus said, "And He will send out His angels with a loud trumpet call, and they will gather His elect from the four winds, from one end of heaven to the other" (Matthew 24:31).

### "Angels from the Realms of Glory"

Angels from the realms of glory,
  Wing your flight o'er all the earth;
Ye who sang creation's story,
  Now proclaim Messiah's birth.

Come and worship, come and worship;
Worship Christ, the newborn King.

(*LSB* 367:1)

**23**

# Mary
### READING: LUKE 1:46–55

And Mary said, "My soul magnifies the Lord, and my spirit rejoices in God my Savior, for He has looked on the humble estate of His servant. For behold, from now on all generations will call me blessed."
(Luke 1:46–48)

Mary, a virgin, humbly accepted the news that the angel Gabriel announced to her. She would be the mother of God, for the child in her womb was conceived by the Holy Spirit. All generations would call her blessed, for from her womb the Savior of the world would be born. With God as His Father and Mary as His mother, Jesus is both true God and true man—true man that He might suffer and die, and true God that He might rise from the dead and that His death would pay for the sins of the whole world.

## "Savior of the Nations, Come"

Savior of the nations, come,
Virgin's Son, make here Your home!
Marvel now, O heav'n and earth,
That the Lord chose such a birth.

Here a maid was found with child,
Yet remained a virgin mild.
In her womb this truth was shown:
God was there upon His throne.

(*LSB* 332:1, 3)

# Hammer

READING: MATTHEW 1:18–25

KEY BIBLE VERSE

But as he considered these things, behold, an angel of the Lord appeared to him in a dream, saying, "Joseph, son of David, do not fear to take Mary as your wife, for that which is conceived in her is from the Holy Spirit. She will bear a son, and you shall call His name Jesus, for He will save His people from their sins." (Matthew 1:20–21)

Joseph, a carpenter, was a just man. He trusted in God when an angel announced to him that Mary's child was conceived by the Holy Spirit. He took Mary to be his wife instead of divorcing her. He provided for and protected Mary and Jesus. He led them to Bethlehem, then to Egypt, and back to Nazareth. The love that Joseph showed as an adoptive father reminds us of the love that our heavenly Father shows to us as His adopted children. The words of 1 John 3:1 remind us, "See what kind of love the Father has given to us, that we should be called children of God; and so we are."

### "Oh, Blest the House"

Oh, blest the parents who give heed
Unto their children's foremost need
And weary not of care or cost.
May none to them and heav'n be lost!

(*LSB* 862:3)

# Sandals
### READING: LUKE 2:1–5

And Joseph also went up from Galilee, from the town of Nazareth, to Judea, to the city of David, which is called Bethlehem, because he was of the house and lineage of David, to be registered with Mary, his betrothed, who was with child.

(Luke 2:4–5)

It was a long, dusty journey to Bethlehem for Mary and Joseph. The sandals remind us of their journey. The journey was a culmination of everything the prophets foretold. The wait for a Savior was over. He would be born in Bethlehem, as foretold by Micah. He would be born into Jesse's family tree, as God had promised to David and as Isaiah had foretold. When Mary and Joseph finished their journey, the Christ Child was born. We have followed the journey of God's promise through Scripture, and when we wake up tomorrow, it will be Christmas morning. The wait is almost over!

### "O Little Town of Bethlehem"

O little town of Bethlehem, How still we see thee lie!
Above thy deep and dreamless sleep The silent stars go by;
Yet in thy dark streets shineth The everlasting light.
The hopes and fears of all the years Are met in thee tonight.

(*LSB* 361:1)

# Manger
### READING: LUKE 2:8–21

And they went with haste and found Mary and Joseph,
and the baby lying in a manger.
(Luke 2:16)

Christmas is here! The wait is over! After weeks of preparation and anticipation, the day has come. It is a day worth celebrating, for God becoming man is momentous. Jesus came humbly, wrapped in swaddling clothes and lying in a manger. Yet a multitude of angels filled the sky in song, and the shepherds praised and glorified God for all they had heard and seen. God's promise to Adam and Eve long ago was fulfilled in Jesus Christ. We have peace and joy this Christmas as we celebrate with the angels, the shepherds, and all the saints.

### "Away in a Manger"

Away in a manger, no crib for a bed,
The little Lord Jesus laid down His sweet head.
The stars in the bright sky looked down where He lay,
The little Lord Jesus asleep on the hay.

The cattle are lowing, the baby awakes,
But little Lord Jesus, no crying He makes.
I love Thee, Lord Jesus! Look down from the sky,
And stay by my cradle till morning is nigh.

Be near me, Lord Jesus; I ask Thee to stay
Close by me forever and love me, I pray.
Bless all the dear children in Thy tender care,
And take us to heaven to live with Thee there.

(*LSB* 365)

# Star
## READING: MATTHEW 2:1–12

**KEY BIBLE VERSE:**

Behold, wise men from the east came to Jerusalem, saying, "Where is He who has been born king of the Jews? For we saw His star when it rose and have come to worship Him."

(Matthew 2:1b–2)

This Advent we have been following the promise of a Savior that God made to Adam and Eve, Abraham, Isaac, and His people Israel. That promise was fulfilled in Jesus Christ. Yet Jesus did not come only for the Jews but also for the Gentiles. The Wise Men followed a star to the place where Jesus lay, and they fell down to worship Him and offered Him expensive gifts. The Wise Men were not Jews, but they knew that Jesus is the King of *all* nations. He came for all people. He is the King of kings and Lord of lords. The wait for Christmas is over, yet as God's people, we are now waiting for the return of our King, Jesus Christ. We wait with anticipation, trusting in God's promise. He will come again in glory and will draw us to Himself. What a glorious day that will be. Come quickly, Lord!

### "Songs of Thankfulness and Praise"

Songs of thankfulness and praise,
Jesus, Lord, to Thee we raise,
  Manifested by the star
  To the sages from afar,
Branch of royal David's stem
In Thy birth at Bethlehem:
  Anthems be to Thee addressed,
  God in man made manifest.

(*LSB* 394:1)

# The Word Became Flesh
### READING: JOHN 1:1–14

And the Word became flesh and dwelt among us, and
we have seen His glory, glory as of the only Son from
the Father, full of grace and truth.

(John 1:14)

At Christmastime, we celebrate the Word becoming flesh, the
birth of Jesus Christ. During this Advent season, we followed the
promise of the Word becoming flesh throughout the Old Testament,
beginning with creation. Yet Jesus Himself was there at creation, in
the beginning. John calls Jesus "the Word." He says, "In the beginning
was the Word, and the Word was with God, and the Word was God"
(John 1:1). Jesus, as true God, has always existed. As we say in the
Nicene Creed, Jesus was "begotten, not made, being of one substance
with the Father, by whom all things were made." Jesus, begotten from
all eternity, true God, full of glory and light, humbled Himself to be
born of a virgin; to become a man; to live, to die, and to rise again.
Why? For you. For all of humanity. The love that God has for us knows
no end. This is love: that while we were still sinners, Christ died for us.

### "O Sing of Christ"

O sing of Christ, whose birth made known
   The kindness of the Lord,
Eternal Word made flesh and bone
   So we could be restored.
Upon our frail humanity
   God's finger chose to trace
The fullness of His deity,
   The icon of His grace.

(*LSB* 362:1)

# The Holy Innocents
### READING: MATTHEW 2:13–23

KEY BIBLE VERSE

Then Herod, when he saw that he had been tricked
by the wise men, became furious, and he sent and
killed all the male children in Bethlehem and in all that
region who were two years old or under, according to
the time that he had ascertained from the wise men.

(Matthew 2:16)

King Herod was an evil man who felt jealous and threatened when
he heard of the new king, baby Jesus. In fury, he ordered that all male
children two years old and younger in Bethlehem be killed. Thankfully,
Joseph had been warned in a dream by an angel of the Lord and
had taken Jesus and Mary to Egypt, where Herod would not be able to
destroy the child. Yet many other children were killed that day. Today
is called the Feast of the Holy Innocents. It is a day to remember and
honor those babies who died by King Herod's order. While Jesus escaped
death by King Herod, He would willingly go to the cross many
years later. His cross would have a sign saying, "King of the Jews."
Herod feared an earthly king, but Jesus came as our heavenly King—
not to conquer kingdoms of this world but to conquer sin and death.
By His blood, those children who died by King Herod's hand—and
all who die in Christ—will surely be raised again to eternal salvation.

### "Sweet Flowerets of the Martyr Band"

Ah, what availed King Herod's wrath?
He could not stop the Savior's path.
  Alone, while others murdered lay,
  In safety Christ is borne away.

(*LSB* 969:3)

# A Great Light

## READING: ISAIAH 9:1–7

### KEY BIBLE VERSE

The people who walked in darkness have seen a great light; those who dwelt in a land of deep darkness, on them has light shone.

(Isaiah 9:2)

When the prophet Isaiah foretold the birth of Christ, he spoke of light illuminating the darkness. This is a common theme throughout Scripture, as the psalmist sang, "Your word is a lamp to my feet and a light to my path" (Psalm 119:105), and as Jesus Himself said, "I am the light of the world. Whoever follows Me will not walk in darkness, but will have the light of life" (John 8:12).

Ever since Adam and Eve disobeyed God in the garden, the darkness of sin and death has loomed over creation. But God, the Creator of light, would not leave His beloved forlorn in darkness. He sent the light of the world, His only Son, to take that spiritual darkness to the cross. Darkness covered the whole land when Jesus died, but the darkness was only temporary, as was Jesus' death. On the third day, He rose again, scattering the darkness and bringing light and life.

### "Savior of the Nations, Come"

From the manger newborn light
Shines in glory through the night.
Darkness there no more resides;
In this light faith now abides.

(*LSB* 332:7)

# Grace upon Grace

READING: JOHN 1:15–18

For from His fullness we have all received,
grace upon grace.

(John 1:16)

"For the law was given through Moses; grace and truth came through Jesus Christ" (John 1:17). The proper distinction of Law and Gospel is crucial to understanding our place in the story of salvation. It is easy to equate the Old Testament with Law, and the New Testament with Gospel. Certainly the Ten Commandments were given through Moses in the Old Testament, and there are many instances of judgment and condemnation. We are incapable of keeping the Law, so the Law always condemns. Yet the Law of God is good and wise, and it prepares the way for the Gospel. There is certainly also Gospel in the Old Testament, as we've followed the Gospel promise. The fullness of the Gospel comes to fruition in the New Testament, through Jesus Christ. Through Him, we receive grace upon grace: overflowing blessings of mercy, wisdom, righteousness, and life everlasting. Christ came not to destroy the Law but to fulfill it. Glory be to Him who fulfilled it perfectly and freely gives to us the salvation He won on the cross.

### "Arise, O Christian People"

Arise, O Christian people! Prepare yourselves today;
Prepare to greet the Savior, Who takes your sins away.
To us by grace alone
  The truth and light were given;
  The promised Lord from heaven
To all the world is shown.

(*LSB* 354:1)

# New Year's Eve

## READING: REVELATION 21:1–8

KEY BIBLE VERSE

And He who was seated on the throne said,
"Behold, I am making all things new."
(Revelation 21:5a)

As we celebrate the end of another calendar year, we recognize that we are already well into the new Church Year. Advent was a time of waiting, just as on New Year's Eve we anticipate what the new year will bring. Many will make resolutions, trying to be better versions of themselves. Some resolutions will stick, but most of them will fail. Christ is the only one who can truly make us new, and He does so through the waters of Holy Baptism. Washed free of sin, united to Christ, we are a new creation. Yet we live in the "now and not yet." As the people of old awaited the coming of the Messiah, we eagerly anticipate His second coming. In the new creation, God will wipe away every tear from our eyes, "and death shall be no more, neither shall there be mourning, nor crying, nor pain anymore, for the former things have passed away" (Revelation 21:4). What joy we have, knowing in full confidence that these words are trustworthy and true!

### "All Christians Who Have Been Baptized"

So use [your Baptism] well! You are made new—
In Christ a new creation!
As faithful Christians, live and do
Within your own vocation,
Until that day when you possess
His glorious robe of righteousness
Bestowed on you forever!

(*LSB* 596:6)

# The Eighth Day
### READING: LUKE 2:21–23

**KEY BIBLE VERSE**

And at the end of eight days, when He was circumcised, He was called Jesus, the name given by the angel before He was conceived in the womb.

(Luke 2:21)

According to the Old Testament law, all male babies were to be circumcised eight days after birth. Jesus began His fulfillment of the law on the eighth day—"the first day of the new week of God's new creation, which will also be the day of the resurrection" (Arthur A. Just Jr., *Luke 1:1–9:50*, Concordia Commentary [St. Louis: CPH, 1996], 118). At the time of His circumcision, Jesus also received His name, which had been given to Him by the angel while He was still in Mary's womb. His name revealed what His destiny would be. *Jesus* means "He will save His people from their sins."

Many baptismal fonts have eight sides to show that Baptism is part of the new creation, the "eighth day." Just as Jesus was named on the eighth day and rose from the tomb on the eighth day, in Baptism we are named as children of the heavenly Father and are given new life. The gift of the eighth day of creation, the new creation, is only given to us because Jesus fulfilled the Law and did exactly as His name proclaims—saved us from our sins.

### "Jesus! Name of Wondrous Love"

Jesus! Name decreed of old,
To the maiden mother told,
Kneeling in her lowly cell,
By the angel Gabriel.

(*LSB* 900:2)

# Two Turtledoves

READING: LUKE 2:22–24

KEY BIBLE VERSE

And when the time came for their purification according to the Law of Moses, they brought Him up to Jerusalem to present Him to the Lord.

(Luke 2:22)

"On the ninth day of Christmas my true love gave to me . . ." Did you know that today is the ninth day of Christmas? The reading today calls to mind that famous Christmas carol, as Mary and Joseph offered a sacrifice of two turtledoves when they went to Jerusalem for Jesus' circumcision and Mary's purification. This did not take place on the ninth day of Christmas but forty days after Jesus' birth. They did not give two turtledoves as a Christmas gift to their true love but as an offering to their true God in order to fulfill the Law of Moses. Of all the sacrifices that could be offered, two turtledoves was the most modest. Mary and Joseph could not afford a more extravagant offering, but in humble obedience they gave what they could. Their humility and faithfulness set an example for the humble and faithful Christ Child, who would one day give us all, His true loves, the gift of salvation by His death on the cross.

### "In His Temple Now Behold Him"

In His temple now behold Him,
 See the long-expected Lord;
Ancient prophets had foretold Him,
 God has now fulfilled His word.
Now to praise Him, His redeemed
 Shall break forth with one accord.

(*LSB* 519:1)

# Simeon's Song
## READING: LUKE 2:25–35

He took Him up in his arms and blessed God and said, "Lord, now You are letting Your servant depart in peace, according to Your word; for my eyes have seen Your salvation that You have prepared in the presence of all peoples, a light for revelation to the Gentiles, and for glory to Your people Israel."

(Luke 2:28–32)

Simeon, a faithful and righteous man, received a precious gift in his old age—the gift of being one of the first to recognize Jesus for who He was: the promised Messiah. The Holy Spirit led him to baby Jesus in the temple, and there Simeon held the child and blessed God. His blessing may be familiar to you; it is called the Nunc Dimittus and can be found in the liturgy. Simeon also blessed Mary and Joseph. He foretold Jesus' death when he told Mary, "a sword will pierce through your own soul also" (Luke 2:35). Mary's soul felt pierced as she watched her son die in agony on the cross. Blood and water poured out when the soldier pierced Jesus, and that life-giving blood and water are now offered to us in Holy Communion and Baptism. By His wounds we are healed, and Mary's devastation was quickly turned to joy on Easter morning.

### "In Peace and Joy I Now Depart"

Christ Jesus brought this gift to me, My faithful Savior,
Whom You have made my eyes to see By Your favor.
Now I know He is my life,
My friend when I am dying.

(*LSB* 938:2)

# Fulfilled Promise

READING: LUKE 2:36–38

And coming up at that very hour she began to give thanks to God and to speak of Him to all who were waiting for the redemption of Jerusalem.

(Luke 2:38)

The prophetess Anna, like Simeon, was faithfully awaiting the promised Messiah. Trusting in God's promises, she worshiped with fasting and prayer, day and night. What joy she must have felt to see the fulfillment of God's promise with her own eyes! At the sight of Jesus, she gave thanks to God and began speaking of Him to all who were waiting for the redemption of Jerusalem. Simeon and Anna were not the only faithful Israelites left, waiting for God to fulfill His promise through Jesus. Many were waiting for the redemption that only Christ could bring. The excitement in the temple that day must have been like no other. The wait was over; the Redeemer was there, God in man made manifest. His redeeming work would offer salvation from sin, death, and the power of the devil—not just for the faithful Israelites but for all mankind.

### "In His Temple Now Behold Him"

In the arms of her who bore Him,
　Virgin pure, behold Him lie
While His aged saints adore Him
　Ere in perfect faith they die.
Alleluia, alleluia!
　Lo, the incarnate God Most High!

(*LSB* 519:2)

# The Days of Old
### READING: ISAIAH 63:7–14

**KEY BIBLE VERSE**

In all their affliction He was afflicted, and the angel of
His presence saved them; in His love and in His pity He
redeemed them; He lifted them up and carried them
all the days of old.

(Isaiah 63:9)

Born into a world full of sin, God's people of old, the Israelites, continued to rebel against Him. Yet God had claimed them as His own, and in their affliction He, too, was afflicted. No matter how many times they left Him, God did not leave them. During the Passover feast, the Israelites would remember what God had done through Moses to save them. God, too, remembered the days of old, and He remembered His promises. He sent His Son, Jesus Christ, to suffer the ultimate affliction by crucifixion.

Just as the Israelites remembered what God had done in the days of old, the Old Testament works of God are still important for Christians. As Stephen, the first martyr, was testifying of God, he recounted God's works in the Old Testament. He recounted how God led His people and kept His promises. Salvation comes through Jesus Christ, but the story of salvation starts in Genesis with the first Gospel promise made to Adam and Eve. We remember the days of old and praise God for His faithfulness throughout all of history.

### "Let Our Gladness Have No End"

Prophesied in days of old, alleluia!
God has sent Him as foretold, alleluia!

On this day God gave us
Christ, His Son, to save us;
Christ, His Son, to save us.

(*LSB* 381:2)

# My Father's House
### READING: LUKE 2:41–52

**KEY BIBLE VERSE**

And He said to them, "Why were you looking for Me?
Did you not know that I must be in My Father's house?"
(Luke 2:49)

As a young boy of twelve, Jesus confirmed that He was, indeed, the Son of God. After they had lost Him for three days, Mary and Joseph found Jesus in the temple. After seeing their distress, Jesus said, "Why were you looking for Me? Did you not know that I must be in My Father's house?" His words show that He understood that He was the Son of God.

Many years later, rather than being lost for three days, Jesus would spend three days in the tomb. The temple curtain would be torn in two, for God would no longer be separated from His people. Jesus' death provides unlimited access to the Father, delivered to us in the waters of Holy Baptism. His resurrection confirms His divinity, and through baptismal waters we are drowned to sin and raised to new life with the risen Lord. The gifts and blessings we receive are overflowing and never-ending. To God be all glory!

### "Built on the Rock"

We are God's house of living stones,
Built for His own habitation.
He through baptismal grace us owns
Heirs of His wondrous salvation.
Were we but two His name to tell,
Yet He would deign with us to dwell
With all His grace and favor.

(*LSB* 645:3)